Paul Elmer More, Bruce Rogers

A century of Indian epigrams, chiefly from the Sanskrit of

Bhartrihari

Paul Elmer More, Bruce Rogers

A century of Indian epigrams, chiefly from the Sanskrit of Bhartrihari

ISBN/EAN: 9783337305383

Printed in Europe, USA, Canada, Australia, Japan

Cover: Foto ©Thomas Meinert / pixelio.de

More available books at **www.hansebooks.com**

A CENTURY OF INDIAN EPIGRAMS

CHIEFLY FROM THE SANSKRIT
OF BHARTRIHARI
BY PAUL ELMER MORE

BOSTON AND NEW YORK
HOUGHTON, MIFFLIN AND COMPANY
The Riverside Press, Cambridge
1899

COPYRIGHT, 1898, BY PAUL ELMER MORE

ALL RIGHTS RESERVED

> "They reckon ill who leave me out;
>   When me they fly, I am the wings;
> I am the doubter and the doubt,
>   And I the hymn the Brahmin sings."

To IRVING BABBITT, Esq.

My dear Babbitt,—So much of what I have learned of Oriental things and have thought about them is associated with your name, that it seems now only natural to offer you this little Oriental book. Let it serve as a memorial to you of our life together in Cambridge, and of our many peripatetic discussions regarding matters sacred and profane,—peripatetic I call them, although, as the poet says, our words often outnumbered our steps and the days set briefer than our theme,

Te mihi iucundas efficiente vias.

The life of the ancient Brahmins was an unfailing subject of argument, and we were fond of comparing their doctrine with the discipline of Buddha. Did we ever come to a conclusion? I think not. And now, as an aftermath of those days, I have attempted in these translations to bring together the verses I used to quote in illustration of my views, or should have quoted if memory had been faithful to her call. And, first of all, do not demur on reading the name of Bhartrihari at the head of these epigrams. Count them up, and you will find the greater part taken from his work, while precedent from India itself justified me in substituting other stanzas where his own were not to my purpose.

As for Bhartrihari, I wish my study enabled me to relate with certainty the story of his life; but it is all dark. This will not surprise you, for perhaps no other people of the world have cared so little for historical record as the Hindus. Their rulers, their lawgivers, their revered sages, are for the most part names only. Even in their more personal literature the individuality of the poet is rarely manifest; and this is a witness to the sincerity of their words who ever proclaimed the surrender of earthly distinctions for the winning of a higher good. Concerning Bhartrihari various traditions may be read. Thus much apparently is true, that at some early period in our era he reigned in Oujein, the legend would add magnificently, to enhance his later renunciation, as in the case of Buddha also. Suddenly he was aroused from this voluptuous life by an intrigue of the palace whose nature tradition detects in one of the epigrams of our collections:

Now judge ye! — for a girl I walked forlorn.

Thereupon he abdicated the throne in favor of a younger brother, and, withdrawing to the woods, passed the remainder of his life in a cavern still pointed out to the curious traveler at Oujein. Here we may picture to ourselves the royal eremite reclined at ease during the cool hours of morning or evening twilight, looking out over the valley land and the dusky city; and we may understand how at times, in the intervals of more austere thought, the recollection of his former life and of the rivalries of busy courtiers may have brought a smile to his lips: —

> How slow to him who haunts preferment's door
> The long days drag! how lightly hurry o'er
> When the awakened soul hath thrown aside
>   Its load of worldly pride!
>
> So, lying near my cavern's rocky ledge,
> I'd dream at ease upon the mountain edge;
> And laugh a little in my heart, and then
>   Plunge into thought again.

Do the English words of this last line seem familiar to you? They are borrowed from a stanza of Matthew Arnold you were fond of quoting : —

> The East bow'd low before the blast
> In patient, deep disdain;
> She let the legions thunder past,
> And plunged in thought again.

Bhartrihari wrote his epigram long ago and in a far-off land, but the sentiment of it is still new. Just recently I read it to a friend who for years had been a miner in the mountains of Colorado. There, in a solitary hut built on a rocky ledge, he passed summer and winter with a single companion, far removed from civilization. "Ay," said he when I had read the verses, "your old Hindu tells the simple truth; every word of it might have been written from my own experience." Such, it is said, were the last years of our poet's life. Nor must we suppose that their isolation oppressed him with a feeling of special loneliness. He was versed in the wisdom of his land, and must well have pondered in his youth the celebrated lines in the law-book, telling of a more universal and inevitable loneliness of the spirit, whether in society or solitude; for it is written : —

> Alone each mortal first draws breath;
> Alone goes down the way of death;
> Alone he tastes the bitter food
> Of evil deeds, alone the fruit of good.

Now this particular tale of the prince and hermit may be true or may not; but that a royal convert should abandon the luxury of his palace, and choose a peaceful life of contemplation in the forest, would be no more than a commonplace of Indian experience. Their moralists indeed, and Bhartrihari among them, speak of the three paths, pleasure, worldly wisdom, and renunciation; but in reality they recognized only two ideals, between which they could conceive no substantial ground of mediation. Our poet states the contrast sharply in one of his epigrams: "There are in the world but two things that men may cherish,— either the youth of fair girls who yearn ever for the renewal of love's dallying, or else the forest-life." And again, after the choice is made, he writes: "Ho, Lord of Love! why weary thy hand with ever twanging the bow? Ho, sweet cuckoo bird! why warble in vain thy amorous songs? And thou, fair girl, turn otherwhere thy sly glances, charged with languorous spells and sweet allurements. Now is my mind plunged in the ambrosia of meditation at Çiva's feet."

We read of Buddha also that he fled from a voluptuous court to seek salvation in the wilderness. They but followed in the steps of innumerable holy men before them. In fact, such a withdrawal from the world was definitely enjoined on every Brahmin after his duties as householder had been performed and his sons had come to maturity. We have only to glance at their ancient books to learn how commonly this precept was obeyed. The Greeks, too, who became acquainted with India under Alexander, came back with marvelous accounts of these forest-dwellers and gymnosophists. It was not so hard in that warm climate to live in the wilderness, fashioning for the body rough garments of bark-fibre, eating of the abundant fruits, drinking the water of unpolluted streams, bathing in the sacred pools, and sleeping on gathered leaves. A village was not far away, and the people were always glad to fill the holy man's bowl with rice and fragments of bread, if he chose to present himself for alms.

Two classes of hermits may be distinguished, — those who practiced austerities, and those who merely sought a place of untroubled retirement. The self-inflicted penance of the former was often incredibly severe. The epics are replete with exaggerated accounts of their endurance. Such is the wild legend of the Sagarids, — of the grandson of Sagara who for thirty-two thousand years devoted himself to austerities on the heights of Himâlaya, and passed to heaven without seeing the accomplishment of his desires; of the great-grandson who with arms raised aloft stood in the midst of four fires and beneath the blazing sun, nourishing himself on fallen leaves, for a thousand years. Then at last the gods were satisfied, and in answer to his prayer sent down the sacred Gangâ, or Ganges, from heaven; whose thunderous fall, the story says, Çiva first received on his head, for otherwise it would have crushed the world. So for many years the river strayed in the matted locks of the god, until, finding an outlet, it poured down on the earth. These are foolish stories, but they indicate very well the ideal which the anchorite held before him. His aim was not so much to atone for sins as to fortify the will by endurance until even the gods must tremble at his word. To counteract the power of these aspirants the gods often gave themselves to similar practices, and Çiva especially is represented as engaging in the most fantastic forms of penance.

But, besides these savage persecutors of virtue, many withdrew to the woods for the sake of undisturbed meditation. Some dwelt alone, like our royal seer, thinking that wisdom is to be courted in solitude. Others took their families with them and lived together in friendly colonies. There the intricacies of the Brahminical ritual might be exchanged for pious contemplation, and the sacrifice in the imagination became as efficacious as the actual offering on the altar. Genial debate gave exercise to the mind, and the cultivation of fruits and flowers might occupy the hands. There is nothing more beautiful, nothing tenderer, in Indian poetry than the portrayal of this forest-life in many famous episodes of the Epics and in the Drama of the Ring.

But to return to Bhartrihari, who chose rather the deeper tranquillity of isolation. Under his name we have a little book of epigrams called the Çataka-trayam, or Century-triad, in which he unfolds in somewhat broken sequence his experience of life. The first hundred stanzas are devoted to the love of woman, her charm and yet her baleful influence. He sings the power and mischievous deeds of Kâma, the Indian Eros, of whom many strange stories are told. Now Kâma was a mighty archer, though his arrows were tipped only with flowers; and often the gods themselves had to lament the fatal accuracy of his aim. He is a mighty angler as well. Women are his bait, and we, poor silly fish, are caught on his hook and then broiled on his fire, — a dainty repast for a god, no doubt.

Of these stanzas devoted to women some are very tender, some very bitter. Those that depict her charms have a peculiarly melting, sympathetic quality such as we find in our romantic poetry. It is indeed worthy of remark that the Hindu treatment of love and nature is in many ways more akin to our own sentiment than are the classics. Love, to be sure, is without the Platonic mania which infests modern poetry, but otherwise is expressed with the same wistful tenderness so familiar to us, and so foreign to the simpler, more virile temper of Greece and Rome. Together with this delicacy there is, however, a marked monotony in the Hindu poets' delineation of women, due to an inevitable habit of generalizing. They write not of a particular woman but of the kind, repeating certain conventional traits of description almost without variation, and treating her, not as an individual character, but as a symbol of sensual pleasure to be flattered or reviled, according to the writer's temperament.

Natural description is introduced not merely to give a locality for the action, as in the classics. It is more closely identified with the mood of the agent, and becomes highly symbolical as in writers like our own Hawthorne. I know that this more intimate feeling for Nature is not entirely wanting in the classics, and that such general distinctions are easily exaggerated. The sea in Homer has a haunting, half mystical affinity with the moods of his heroes. We remember the priest of Apollo walking in silence by the shore of the many-sounding sea. We remember that Achilles was the child of an ocean goddess, and see him in his wrath before his hut looking out over the tumultuous waters. Odysseus, when we first meet him, is sitting on the beach, after his wont, gazing homeward over the unharvested sea, wasting his heart with tears and lamentations. And throughout the poem, to the last prophecy that his rest is to come after establishing the worship of Poseidon in a far inland country, always the ocean is interwoven with his destiny. In both poems the "murmurs and scents of the infinite sea" are never far away, and we cannot think of Homer's world without repeating his words: —

περὶ δὲ ῥόος Ὠκεανοῖο
ἀφρῷ μορμύρων ῥέεν ἄσπετος.

In Lucretius the sky, the *flammantia mœnia mundi*, seems with its unspeakable terrors and infinite distances, "traversed by the moon and the day, by the night with her austere constellations, by night-wandering torches of heaven and flitting fires, by clouds, sun, rains, snow, winds, lightnings, hail, by swift shuddering sounds and mighty murmuring of threats," — the sky seems ever to stand as the physical counterpart of the poet's own titanic thought, striving to note with mortal speech immortal things. Virgil, too, might be adduced for his use of the glad meadows and the works of men; but, after all, this symbolic treatment of the outer world is sufficiently rare in antiquity to justify our comparison. The classical writers did not as a rule search for this sympathetic spirit in

Nature, nor read in her varying aspects the expression of their own changeful moods. But in Indian poetry it is quite different. Here the world loses its firm reality and seems but a shadow of the inner man. Nor is it a wilful paradox to assert that because of this very unreality of nature the Hindu's feeling for it becomes in a way more intensely real: his contact with it is closer and more sympathetic, just because it is a mere projection of his own personality. One need only read the first Century of Bhartrihari to see how in this respect Indian poetry approaches the methods of mediæval romance. Nature is here burdened with human meaning; birds and flowers, hills, sky, winds, and streams, all the earth is redolent of passion. In the springtide the song of the cuckoo brings torture to those who are separated; the lotus flower multiplies in a myriad places one beloved countenance; the açoka tree may not open its swelling buds until touched by a maiden's foot.

The second Century is perhaps less interesting than either of the other two. Its subject is the prudential ethics of worldly wisdom, pointed now and then with sarcastic flings at fools, flatterers, pedants, and all babblers; elevated at times to the expression of the highest and purest morality; and troubled again with bitter reflections on the brevity and insufficiency of mortal existence.

There is a marked change on turning to the third and last Century. We feel at once that here the poet's heart is in his work when he sings of the true wisdom, of the finding of peace, and the gladness of his new life. To characterize these stanzas would be to review the ideals of Hindu philosophy, and it is better to allow Bhartrihari to speak for himself. One principle, and that the fundamental one, of their religion, let me touch upon briefly, because it is commonly overlooked or perverted in systematic treatises on the subject. We read constantly of the monism of the Hindus, of their attempts to reduce all things to one substance. But this statement must be accepted with a reservation. In fact their intellectual attitude is the result of a keen perception of the dual nature of man and the world at large; and this holds true even in the Vedânta, commonly cited as the most radical of monistic systems. Furthermore, it would hardly be too much to aver that the spirituality of any philosophy or religion is measured by its recognition of this contrast. The Iranians, nearest of kin to the Hindus, divided the universe into two eternally hostile camps, the *regnum lucis* and the *regnum tenebrarum*, which forever clash in battle. And man, as containing in himself both elements, must bear a part in the ceaseless conflict. Saint Augustine cannot emphasize too strongly the heinousness of sin, — sin, not eternal in its nature nor yet a product of the body, but the aberration of a free finite will that denies allegiance to its creator, the source of life, and whose penalty is death. Plato, speaking for Greece and transcending its old philosophy, traces the discord of existence to the opposition of spirit and matter; and this, likewise, is the theory of the Hindus. They proclaim the irreconcilable enmity of the soul and the body. Salvation with them, as with the Greek, is a system of purgation, a dying to the flesh, until the soul is made free to enjoy its own unalloyed perfection. Plato affirms that we can have knowledge only of the soul and of essences similar to the soul; touching the body and material things, there is only ignorance, or at best uncertain opinion. He is fond of identifying knowledge and virtue, ignorance and vice, and of avowing that by knowledge the wise man liberates himself from the world,— but knowledge of what? Hardly in Plato will you find an adequate answer to this simple and inevitable question. Now the Vedânta teaches the same doctrine of knowledge and ignorance; but it goes a step further, and herein lie its clearness and originality. Regarding the world without, we have only ignorance or false opinion. It therefore exists for us only in these, and for us ignorance is the cause of the world. With the acquisition of knowledge ignorance is destroyed, and the world of which it is the cause ceases for us to exist. We win deliverance by knowledge,— and knowledge of what? By apprehension of this definite truth, that the soul has real existence, and that the world has only a phantom existence in illusion. Knowledge, it may be added, is not a verbal conviction merely, but something akin to faith, a realization of truth that touches the whole character of man, springing up of itself by some strange incommunicable force.

Such in brief is the aspiration that pervades Sanskrit literature, and that finds expression in these epigrams of Bhartrihari. It would be a satisfaction to know that they really contain the meditations of the princely recluse of Oujein; but unfortunately they are preserved in so disorderly a sequence, differing too so widely in various recensions, and so many stanzas have been substituted or added to the original three hundred, that doubts arise regarding the authenticity of the whole collection. Either Bhartrihari's name has been loosely given to a floating anthology, as the name of Solomon was similarly employed by the Jews, or else a long succession of editors have altered and added without scruple. For my own part I find in the greater number of these poems so peculiar a flavor, something so distinct from the other thousands of epigrams in Boehtlingk's Anthology, that I accept without hesitation their traditional origin. Out of them I have selected for translation a number which seem to contain the best expression of the poet's ideas, and in lieu of explanatory notes have added stanzas from other sources, freely, having regard to the mixed and uncertain nature of the Sanskrit collection.

And now, my dear Babbitt, with these words of introduction to you and to the public, I would place the little book in your hands. You will look in vain for any reproduction of the delicate art, the subtle intricacies of rhythm, the interwoven assonances, the curiously wrought style, of the original. Our language is not capable of these, and must compensate them by artifices of its own. Let me hope that some echo of Bhartrihari's wisdom and pathos may still be heard in this English version.

Accept the volume also as a partial answer to the question often discussed between us, whether the Occident would find enlightenment or only deeper confusion of mind from the study of India and her religious life. By some strange gift of fate, a few nations in the past have accomplished a work once for all and not to be repeated. It is not likely that another people shall arise like the Greeks of the Periclean age, who shall possess so keen a sense of harmony in form and action. A solitary man or group of men may now and then be found whose mind like theirs is attuned to beauty, but we shall look and wait in vain for such another generation. Many things in their life we may censure, may account worthy even of abomination, but one perfect gift they had from their gods. Their forms have passed away with their civilization, and cannot be revived or imitated; but whoever would seek inspiration in art and poetry at their fountain head must now and always turn back to Athens and laboriously learn her ancient speech. So, too, of the Romans we may say that hardly shall the earth bear a second time men of character and temper like these. They have taught us, once for all, what the human will can do. May we not add of the Hindus that for one brief period in their development, during that century when Zoroaster was teaching in Irania and Pythagoras in the West, they showed in their discourse and in their lives a depth of religious sentiment, a grasp of things spiritual, that still after so many ages affects us with wonder, perhaps incredulity, —

"And many are amazed and many doubt"?

We cannot to-day — it is better so — reproduce the literature of Greece; we should shudder at the Roman sternness; to call ourselves disciples of Buddha or believers in Brahma — as some unstable minds are prone to do — would be superstition and not spirituality: yet to each of these peoples we may turn for strength and consolation;

nay, we must turn to them if we would fortify our isolated life with the virtue and dignity of experience.

Bhartrihari wrote at a time when the thought of India had already become stereotyped, and verbal repetition had begun to take the place of living inspiration. He has in him something of his age; we feel at times that the spirit is deadened by the "sad mechanic exercise of verse." On the other hand, no earlier poet can be found whose work has sufficient perfection of form to admit of acceptable translation. Take him all in all, he may stand as no unfaithful exponent of a literature the discussion of which gave so much pleasure, and I trust profit, to our life together in Cambridge : —

Quare habe tibi quidquid hoc libelli.

P. E. M.

SHELBURNE, N. H.
 1 December, 1897.

INDIAN EPIGRAMS

I

One walketh in Renunciation's way;
Another fain would pay
In Worldly Wisdom all his soul's large debt;
And one in Pleasure's path
With love still wandering on would all forget:—
Three roads the wide world hath.

II

In many a cavern on the wild hill-slopes
That near to heaven climb,
By many a pool, dwell eremites with hopes
That laugh at measured time.

They lave in the cool Gangâ where it flows
Over the level rocks;
They peer among the trees where Çiva goes
Tossing his matted locks;

They breathe in joy : but we — alas that fate
Made woman's love so fair!
For love restrains us in a world we hate,
Cajoled by woman's snare.

III

Girls with the startled eyes of forest deer,
And fluttering hands that drip
With sandal-water; bathing-halls with clear
Deep pools to float and dip;

The light moon blown across the shadowy hours,
Cool winds, and odorous flowers,
And the high terraced roof, — all things enhance
In Summer love's sweet trance.

IV

This sodden air a needle scarce would prick;
The wind dies in a gloom
Of dripping leaves; and the low clouds with quick
Reverberations boom.

Bewildered by heaven's fire I blindly grope
Through the chill Autumn storm,
To love's bright chamber, where one heart, I hope,
With summer still is warm.

V

This Winter gale will play the gallant lover,
And meeting careless girls
Will pluck their gowns, and with rude fingers hover
Among their tangled curls.

He'll kiss their eyelids too, their cheeks caress
Till they are all a-tremble;
He'll tease their lips till murmurs soft confess
The love they would dissemble.

VI

'T is earth's Renewal: now the fluttering breeze,
Blown from the snowy hills
And filtered through the blooming mango trees,
The world with sweetness fills.

Now the mad bees are stung with brisk alarm;
And the wild cuckoos charm
The woods with singing, *Well! ah well! 't is
 well!*
We yield to Kâma's spell!

VII

The silvery laughter; eyes that sparkle bold,
Or droop in virgin rue;
The prattling words of wonder uncontrolled
When world and life are new;

The startled flight and dallying slow return,
And all their girlish sport; —
Ah me, that they time's ruinous truth must learn,
Their flowering be so short!

VIII

Who hath escaped desire?
And thou, O King, — what profit in thy wealth
When Time with creeping stealth
Has quenched thy youth and covered o'er love's
    fire?

Nay, let us haunt the hall
Where loves forever call,
And girls with full-blown eyes like lotus flowers
Look laughing into ours,
Ere age and withering palsies blight us all.

IX

A flower whose fragrance none hath savored,
A singing bird no ear hath favored,
White pearl no jeweler hath bored,
Untasted honey freshly stored
In a clean jar, unbroken fruit
That ripens now from virtue's root, —
Wondering I ask, O form unspotted,
To whose delight, sweet girl, thou art allotted?

X

My love within a forest walked alone,
All in a moonlit dale;
And here awhile she rested, weary grown,
And from her shoulders threw the wimpled veil
To court the little gale.

I peering through the thicket saw it all,
The yellow moonbeams fall,
I saw them mirrored from her bosom fly
Back to the moon on high.

XI

O fair Açoka-tree, with love's own red
Thy boughs are all aflame;
Whither, I pray thee, hath my wanton fled?
This way I know she came.

In vain thy nodding in the wind, thy sigh
Of ignorance assumed;
I know because my flower-love wandered by
For joy thy branches bloomed.

I know thee: ever with thy buds unblown,
Till touched by maiden's foot;
And thou so fair — one fairest maid alone
Hath trod upon thy root.

XII

Love's fruit in all the world is only this,
That two as one should think;
And they that disagree yet woo love's bliss,
Dead corpse with corpse would link.

XIII

Pluck the new-budding jasmine flower, and wreathe
A garland for my brows ;
Let saffron on my flesh and sandal breathe
Their perfume of carouse ;
And then, O true love, lean upon my heart,
And all of heaven is there, or the best part.

XIV

Brightly the hearth-fire leap, and the lit lamp
Be burning clear and high;
Let sun or moon and starry hosts encamp
With beacons in the sky : —
Yet darkness in my heart and all is dark,
Till I behold thine eyes and their love-spark.

XV

But to remember her my heart is sad,
To see her is to know
Bewildered thoughts, and touching driveth mad, —
How is she dear that worketh only woe?

XVI

A traveler pausing at the village well,
His hollowed palms a cup,
Bends down to drink, but caught as by a spell,
With thirst unslaked looks up.

And the fair keeper of the fountain stands,
Her girlish laughter stilled,
Nor careth from her urn into his hands
How thin a stream is spilled.

XVII

" Why, pretty fool, art thou so slender grown?
Thou tremblest? and the prize
Of all thy roses, whither is it flown?"

" My Lord, it meaneth nothing," she replies,
And smiles, — but when alone,
Loosing the tears upgathered in her eyes,
Poor fool, she sighs and sighs.

XVIII

With one they laugh and chatter, yet beguile
With luring eyes a second;
A third they cherish in their heart the while, —
Their true love who hath reckoned?

XIX

Now judge ye ! — For a girl I walked forlorn
Who laughed my vows to scorn ;
She loved another, who in coin repaid
Wooing a second maid.

And she, this second, making all complete,
Would worship at my feet. —
Four pretty fools and Kâma with his malice
Thus drove me from my palace.

XX

Harder than faces in a glass designed,
A woman's heart to bind;
Like mountain paths up cragged heights that twist,
Her ways are lightly missed.

Like early dew-drops quivering on a leaf,
Her thoughts are idly brief;
And errors round her grow, as on a vine
The poison-tendrils twine.

XXI

The sportive Love-god in this worldly sea
Angles continually;
And women are his hook, their luring lips
The bait that bobs and dips.

We greedy fools, like silly nibbling fish,
Are landed with a swish;
And then, alack! to end the cruel game
Are broiled on love's quick flame.

XXII

O Wanderer Heart! avoid that haunted grove,
The body of thy love;
Nor in her bosom stray, wild mountain fells
Where Love, the robber, dwells.

XXIII

Fair is her body as a lonely river
Whereon the moonbeams quiver;
About her waist three furrows in a row,
Like circling billows, go.

And there two swans their snowy plumage lave,
Soft riding on the wave;
There water-lilies nodding — 't is her brow,
A whiter flower. — O Thou

That shudderest in this sea of life to sink,
Beware that river-brink:
Lo, in the darkness, in the depths, there dwell
Monsters unnamable.

XXIV

In woman is the cause of shame,
For woman burneth hatred's flame,
Through woman in this body's snare
The soul is mewed,—of woman, ah! beware.

XXV

Who reared this labyrinth of doubt,
This leaguered town of reel and rout,
This house of scandal? who hath sown
These fields where noisome weeds spring up
    alone?

This wizard's basket who hath stored
With all the conjurer's magic hoard
Of vain illusions? — and the soul
But looking once forgets her blissful goal.

This barrier in the heavenly path,
This gateway to the pit of wrath,
Who made her then? what hand perverse
Her moulded, man's inevitable curse?

XXVI

Communion with the good is friendship's root,
    That dieth not until our death;
And on the boughs hang ever golden fruit:—
    And this is friendship, the world saith.

Ourselves we doubt, our hearts we hardly know,
    We lean for guidance on a friend;
Ay, on a righteous man we'd fain bestow
    Our faith, and follow to the end.

XXVII

Like as the shadows of the twilight hour
Differ from those at morn,
So doth a good man's friendship in its power
From that of evil born : —
One small at first still stronger, deeper grows,
One shortens to the close.

XXVIII

By truth the righteous guide upon his course
The rolling sun, and stay the earth by force
    Of penitence austere.
They are the refuge of the worlds outworn,
And worlds that lurk in darkness still are born
    Because they tarry here.

XXIX

A friend or stranger comes he? — so
   They reckon of the narrow mind;
But some of broader reason know
   In all the world one kith and kind.

XXX

Lightly an ignorant boor is made content,
And lightlier yet a sage;
But minds by half-way knowledge warped and bent,
Not Brahma's self their fury may assuage.

XXXI

Oil from the sand a man may strain,
If chance he squeeze with might and main;
The pilgrim at the magic well
Of the mirage his desert thirst may quell.

So traveling far a man by luck
May find a hare horned like a buck; —
But who by art may straighten out
The crooked counsels of a stubborn lout?

XXXII

Better, I said, in trackless woods to roam
  With chattering apes or the dumb grazing herds,
Than dwell with fools, though in a prince's home,
  And bear the dropping of their ceaseless words.

XXXIII

The god hath wove for ignorance a cloak
That he who will may wear;
And mantled thus amid the wisest folk
Fools may unchallenged fare: —
Be silent! over all that words afford,
   Silence hath its reward.

XXXIV

I saw an ass who bore a load
Of sandal wood along the road,
And almost with the burden bent,
Yet never guessed the sandal scent;
So pedants bear a ponderous mass
Of books they comprehend not, — like the ass.

XXXV

Wisdom acquire and knowledge hive,
As thou a thousand years mightst thrive;
For virtue toil with sleepless care,
As Death already grasped thee by the hair.

XXXVI

Say thou what kindly is and truth,
Say not the true that wakens ruth,
Say not the kind that is not sooth.

Yet rather silence were preferred,
And second truth, and the law third,
And only fourth the kindly word.

XXXVII

Where patience dwells what need of other shield?
Why prate of foemen when to wrath we yield?
　More warmth our kindred give than fires; and friends
Far more than soothing herbs our wounds have healed.

Why pray the gods whose heaven by love is wrought?
Why slave for wealth when wisdom is unbought?
　What pearls can modesty adorn? what gift
Of kings add splendor to the poet's thought?

XXXVIII

One law there is : no deed perform
To others that to thee were harm ;
And this is all, all laws beside
With circumstances alter or abide.

XXXIX

Better from the sheer mountain-top
Headlong thy ruined body drop;
Better appease the serpent's ire
With thy right hand; or in the fire
Behold thy riven members tost,
Than once thy mind's integrity were lost.

XL

This have I done, and that will do,
And this half-done must carry through : —
So busied, bustling, full of care,
Poor fools, Death pounces on us unaware.

To-day is thine, fulfill its work,
Let no loose hour her duty shirk;
Still ere thy task is done, comes Death,
The Finisher, — he ends it with thy breath.

XLI

Unworthy be the toil-polluted world of sense,
Ay, hateful as the camping-ground of all offense;
   Yet even in the truth-devoted heart, anon
Breaks forth its vast unnamed impetuous vehe-
      mence.

XLII

The rooted trees would walk ; the beast
  For utterance yearning still is dumb;
  Man toils for some far heaven, wherefrom
The enthronèd gods were fain released.

XLIII

Pleasure of life we have not known,
Ourselves the sport of Fate alone;
Penance of soul we never sought,
But in our heart unbidden sorrows wrought.

Time hath not journeyed, — nay,
But we are passing day by day;
And the desires that still their rage
Are not grown old — ourselves are chilled with age.

XLIV

   For buried treasures earth I bored,
   I smelted all a mountain's hoard,
   I crossed the outrageous boisterous seas,
And for a king's content I sold my ease.

   By night I haunted the foul tomb
   With spells to waken from their doom
   The sleepers. — Did I e'er succeed
A farthing ? — out upon thee, cursèd Greed !

XLV

O'er perilous mountain roads with pain
I've journeyed, yet acquired no gain;
The pride of birth I have forsworn
And toiled in service, yet no profit borne.

In strange homes where I blushed to go
My food I've taken, like the crow,
And eaten shame. — Oh lust of gold!
Oh Greed! that younger grow'st as I wax old!

XLVI

Read! — the Creator's finger on thy brow
Hath wrote the figure of thy wealth; nor thou
In lonely desert hid shalt make it less,
Nor greater on the Golden Mount possess.
What worry then? why in the crowded mart
With vulgar traffic wear away thy heart?
The pitcher at the well is filled, nor more
    Draws at the ocean-shore.

XLVII

A captive snake half dead with fright
Starved in a basket; till one night
A silly mouse, who roamed abroad,
A hole straight through the wicker gnawed,
And in his very gullet jumped.
The serpent felt his thin sides plumped,
Took cheer, and wriggled out in turn. —
Who knows all lucky falls in Fortune's urn?

XLVIII

An old man bald as a copper pot,
Because one noon his head grew hot,
Crawled to a spreading bilva-tree
To seek the shade. By Fate's decree
A fruit just then came tumbling down,
And cracked the old man's brittle crown
With loud explosion — which was worse. —
Ill dogs us everywhere when Fate's averse.

XLIX

I see a dog — no stone to shy at him ;
   Yonder a stone — no dog's in view :
There is your dog, here stones to try at him —
   The king's dog ! what's a man to do ?

L

If the Creator moulding goodly man
   A pearl designed him to adorn the earth,
   And then so fragile made that at the birth
It breaketh,— whose the folly of the plan?

LI

Rather this World forever as a wheel
   Itself revolveth: sure, no guilty hand
   Propelled it, nor shall any bid it stand,
Nor any wit a primal cause reveal.

And thou, my Soul, the same unlaureled race
   Art dragging on through weary change of form;
   Nay, if to-day thou murmur in the storm,
Blame yesterday and choose to-morrow's place.

LII

Like as our outworn garments we discard,
And other new ones don;
So doth the Soul these bodies doff when marred,
And others new put on.

Fire doth not kindle It, nor sword divides,
Nor winds nor waters harm;
Eternal and unchanged the One abides,
And smiles at all alarm.

LIII

Like as a goldsmith beateth out his gold
To other fashions fairer than the old,
    So may the Spirit, learning ever more,
In ever nobler forms his life infold.

LIV

The harvest ripens as the seed was sown,
And he that scattered reaps alone; —
So from each deed there falls a germ
That shall in coming lives its source affirm.

UNSEEN they call it, for it lurks
The hidden spring of present works;
UNKNOWN BEFORE, even as the fruit
Was undiscovered in the vital root.

And he that now impure hath been
Impure shall be, the clean be clean;
We wrestle in our present state
With bonds ourselves we forged, — and call it
Fate.

LV

Before the Gods we bend in awe,
But lo, they bow to fate's dread law:
Honor to Fate, then, austere lord!
But lo, it fashions but our works' reward.

Nay, if past works our present state
Engender, what of gods and fate?
Honor to Works! in them the power
Before whose awful nod even fate must cower.

LVI

These dear companionships are not forever;
  The wheel of being without end
Still whirls: if on the way some meet and sever,—
  'T is brother, mother, father, friend.

LVII

Our little wit is all to blame,
And separation's but a name;
Else would our sorrow day by day
Grow deeper. — Lo, how swift it slips away!

For as a log at random tost
On the wide waves perchance is crost
Here by another drifting spar, —
So on this sea of life our meetings are.

LVIII

    Wayfarers on the dusty road
    By shaded wells their heavy load
    Undoing rest awhile, and then
Pass on restored. — What cause of tears, O men?

LIX

Like as a dancing-girl to sound of lyres
Delights the king and wakens sweet desires
   For one brief hour, and having shown her art
With lingering bow behind the scene retires:

So o'er the Soul alluring Nature vaunts
Her lyric spell, and all her beauty flaunts;
   And she, too, in her time withdrawing leaves
The Watcher to his peace — 't is all she wants.

LX

Now have I seen it all! the Watcher saith,
And wonders that the pageant lingereth:
    And, He hath seen me! then the Other cries,
And wends her way: and this they call the Death.

No more the Spirit feels, no more resolves;
Yet as the potter's wheel awhile revolves
    After the potter's hand is still, awhile
The body draws the breath, and then dissolves.

LXI

I wonder that the wingèd soul
Entered the body's hard control;
I wonder not when worn by age
The prisoned bird escapes the open cage.

LXII

While other birds at will may go
Where the free winds of heaven blow,
You, silly prattler, as the wage
Of your sweet singing, languish in a cage.

LXIII

This World is blind to us that blinds the Soul;
    We find Illusion lord of all its laws,
    We call our Ignorance its inner cause,
And Knowledge trust to break its long control.

Our Self we know, the knower and the known,
    We name it Soul, we worship it as God;
    This Knowledge is the Lord, and at its nod
This We shall pass, and I remain alone.

LXIV

Here nothing is, and nothing there,
And nothing fronts me wheresoe'er;
And reckoning all I find the whole
Mere nothing, nothing — save the reckoning
    soul.

LXV

Seated within this body's car
The silent Self is driven afar;
And the five senses at the pole
Like steeds are tugging restive of control.

And if the driver lose his way,
Or the reins sunder, who can say
In what blind paths, what pits of fear
Will plunge the chargers in their mad career?

Drive well, O Mind, use all thy art,
Thou charioteer! — O feeling Heart,
Be thou a bridle firm and strong!
For the Lord rideth and the way is long.

LXVI

HE, in that solitude before
The world was, looked the wide void o'er
And nothing saw, and said, Lo I
Alone!—and still we echo the lone cry.

Thereat He feared, and still we fear
In solitude when naught is near:
And, Lo, He said, myself alone!
What cause of dread when second is not known?

LXVII

Alone each mortal first draws breath;
Alone goes down the way of death;
Alone he tastes the bitter food
Of evil deeds, alone the fruit of good.

They cast him in the earth away,
They leave him as a lump of clay,
They turn their faces, they are sped,
And only Virtue follows, — he is dead.

So garner Virtue till the end
As 't were our only guide and friend;
With it alone, when all is lost,
We cross the darkness, ah, so hardly crost.

LXVIII

Time is the root of all this earth;
These creatures, who from Time had birth,
Within his bosom at the end
Shall sleep; Time hath nor enemy nor friend.

All we in one long caravan
Are journeying since the world began;
We know not whither, but we know
Time guideth at the front, and all must go.

Like as the wind upon the field
Bows every herb, and all must yield,
So we beneath Time's passing breath
Bow each in turn, — why tears for birth or death?

LXIX

A hundred years we barely keep,
Yet half of this is lost in sleep;
And half our waking time we spend
In the child's folly and the old man's end.

And of the hours remaining, fears
And gaunt disease and parting tears
Are all the prize : — fie on the slave
Who life more values than a bubbling wave!

LXX

A while the helpless wailing child,
A while the youth by lusts defiled,
A while for gold to cringe and swink,
A while to hear the yellow counters clink:

A while of lonely eld's disgrace,
The palsied limb and wizened face, —
Then like the player he too creeps
Behind the heavy curtain — he too sleeps.

LXXI

Fallen our father, fallen who bore
For us the pangs — they went before :
And some with our years grew, but they,
They too now tread on memory's dusty way.

And we ourselves from morn to morn
Now shiver like old trees forlorn
Upon a sandy shore, and all
Our care the lapping waves that haste our fall.

LXXII

Old age like as a tiger held at bay
Still crouches ; sly diseases day by day
   Our leaguered body sap ;
As water from a broken urn, so leak
Our wasting minutes ; — lo, this people seek
   Oblivion in love's lap.

LXXIII

Others for buried friends lament,
Or sigh for wealth too quickly spent:
Fret not, O King; thy own grief call
Part of the fatal grief that toucheth all.

LXXIV

When like an arrow in the dark
Sorrow hath made our breast her mark,
Piercing the mail 'twixt link and link,
One balm there is, one salve: just not to think.

LXXV

Now Sorrow like a threefold chain
Grapples our heart with triple pain :
And one, the strongest bond I think,
Ourselves we forge and rivet link by link.

Another many-fingered Chance
Still weaves with daily circumstance;
And one some strange malignant Might
Drops clanking round us from an unknown height.

LXXVI

Dear brother, I have found the way
Though steep and narrow : and they say
Of old 't was trod by many a seer
Who knew his end and climbed from sphere to sphere.

Searching my heart I found the clue,
One truth though nothing else be true : —
Sorrow within us and without,
And Sorrow nearer clinging when we doubt.

From yonder pure celestial height
Flooding our path a wondrous light
Pours on us; and where'er we go,
This haunting shadow of ourselves we throw.

So be it: if along the track
On Sorrow still we turn our back,
We too may climb to that high doom
With light before us and behind the gloom.

LXXVII

Fear troubles pleasure lest it sap our health;
Fear marreth beauty for the hideous stealth
   Of love; fear prophesies to pride her fall;
Fear palsies strength, and warns the loss of
   wealth.

Fear poisons learning for another's fame;
Fear haunts the flesh with dissolution's shame;
   Fear is to live;—save when the soul with-
      drawn
Looks out and laughs at the world's care and
   claim.

LXXVIII

All dearest things forsake us: — wealth is sped
To-day, or yet to-morrow love lies dead,
   Or hope fades in a year.
Poor fools! what matter when they go or how?
Poor fools! that cling and will not leave them now,
   Adding to loss a fear.
For if themselves they part what pangs they leave!
Nay, fling them forth, and the soul's peace receive,
   Eternal now and here.

LXXIX

Life like the billow rolls, and youthful bloom
Finds in a day its doom;
Wealth fleeter is than fancy; pleasure's lash
Is but the lightning flash;
And these dear arms that hold our neck, beguile
Ah, but a little while : —
Rest then the heart in Brahma till we cross
This sea of being where all errors toss.

LXXX

Like an uneasy fool thou wanderest far
Into the nether deeps,
Or upward climbest where the dim-lit star
Of utmost heaven sleeps.

Through all the world thou rangest, O my soul,
Seeking and wilt not rest;
Behold, the peace of Brahma, and thy goal,
Hideth in thine own breast.

LXXXI

Idle thy wanderings, O my Heart! and all
Thy labor vainly spent;
By weight of inner destiny doth befall
Or faileth each event.

Bear not the burthen of a world outworn,
Nor to the future bow;
With every hour thy joy be newly born,
And earth be new-created every morn, —
Thy life is here and now.

LXXXII

No longer in this haunted jungle roam
With way-worn stumbling feet;
Seek now the safer path that leadeth home,
Turn to thy last retreat.

Rest in the World's still heart; thy little cares
Like wind-rocked billows roll,
And all thy pleasure as the light wind fares; —
Now give thee peace, my soul!

LXXXIII

Of old fair Learning served the wise to ward
Time's grieving from the heart;
Then to the worldly bowed her to afford
The charms of sensual art;
Now each new lordling of an ill-got field
Disdains her; she must yield,
And deeper hides and farther draws apart.

LXXXIV

Say not the words, " 'T is I ! 't is mine ! "
They are the fatal seed
Of future lives upspringing like a weed.

Say rather, " 'Tis not I ! not mine ! "
New life from old desire
Still flames, — withhold the fuel, and where 's the
      fire ?

LXXXV

Before that peaceful Light whose form sublime
Is purest thought uncurbed of space or time,
Before that Light I bow, whose deathless source
    Is self-communing force.

LXXXVI

Within this body side by side
Death and eternity abide;
And death from error grows, but life
The spirit wrings from truth with hourly strife.

LXXXVII

The Seer enlightened lays apart
Follies that dizzy the child heart,
And upward turns his steps to climb
The terraced heights of Wisdom. There sublime

He stands and unperturbed looks down
Upon the far-off swarming town,
Sees the bent farmers till the soil
Like burrowing ants, and wonders at their toil.

LXXXVIII

One boasted : " Lo, the earth my bed,
This arm a pillow for my head,
The moon my lantern, and the sky
Stretched o'er me like a purple canopy.

" No slave-girls have I, but all night
The four winds fan my slumbers light." —
And I astonished : Like a lord
This beggar sleeps ; what more could wealth afford ?

LXXXIX

Are there no caverns in the mountains left?
Are all the forest boughs of leaves bereft
And mellowing fruit? are the wild cataracts still
    On every lonely hill?

Why haunt the servile press? or cringe and bow
To win the nod of some majestic brow
That wears for honor the low insolence
    Of wealth — how got and whence?

XC

Of old they say this holy Gangâ stream
Rolled in the heavenly fields her crystal dream,
And thence by prayer of saintly men was led
    To pour on Çiva's head.

Awhile within the great god's matted locks
She wandered, till the high Himâlayan rocks
Received her thunderous fall; forever thence
    Seaward she rolls immense.

XCI

O World! I faint in this thy multitude
Of little things and their relentless feud;
No meaning have I found through all my days
    In their fantastic maze.

O World! still through the hours of blissful night
The widowed moon her benison of light
Outpoureth, where the sacred river seems
    From heaven to bear sweet dreams.

How soon, O World! beside the Gangâ shore
Through the long silent night shall I implore
The mystic name? how soon in Gangâ's wave
    My sin-stained body lave?

XCII

Is there no pleasure in these palace halls,
Where love invites and music ever calls?
No pleasure, when the revelers troop away,
    If one, the loveliest, stay?

Yet have the prudent weighed the world as froth;
Lo, as a candle-flame by wing of moth
Is fluttered, so they count its fickle mood;
    They turn to solitude.

XCIII

Dear Heart, I go a journey, yet before
Would speak this counsel, for I come no more:
One love our life had, yet a greater still
    The Spirit must fulfill.

Not now the wife is dear for love of wife,
But for the Self; and this our golden life
For life no more we treasure, it is dear
    For that the Self dwells here.

And this beguiling world, the starry dome
Of purple and the gods who call it home,
Man, beast, and flowers that blow and blowing
    perish,
    Not for themselves we cherish,

But for the Self.   And this is love, and they
Who look for other on the lonely way
Are still forsaken. — Tremble not, dear Heart!
  Love stays though I depart.

XCIV

Courage, my Soul! now to the silent wood
Alone we wander, there to seek our food
In the wild fruits, and woo our dreamless sleep
    On soft boughs gathered deep.

There loud authority in folly bold,
And tongues that stammer with disease of gold,
And murmur of the windy world shall cease,
    Nor echo through our peace.

XCV

These trodden lands are everywhere the haunt
Of wilder tribes than any crime may daunt;
And haply some malignant poison-barb
    May pierce thy plumèd garb.

O silly parrot, in the secret boughs
Where peril may not find thee, make thy house:
Come, cease thy prattle, seal thy mouth at length,
    Silence is all thy strength.

XCVI

Who is the Brahmin? — Not the mother's womb
Declares him, nor the robes that all assume;
But the true heart that never greed beguiles,
    Nor turbid lust defiles.

Who is the Brahmin? — He who trembleth not
When snaps the cord that bound to human lot,
Who losing all is glad, whose peace is known
    Unto himself alone.

XCVII

How slow to him who haunts preferment's door
The long days drag! how lightly hurry o'er,
When the awakened soul hath thrown aside
    Its load of worldly pride!

So, lying near my cavern's rocky ledge,
I'd dream at ease upon the mountain edge;
And laugh a little in my heart, and then
    Plunge into thought again.

XCVIII

Fire is the Brahmin's god; the seer
Knows in his heart the godhead near;
Fools have their idol; but the clear
Untroubled vision sees him there and here.

XCIX

Through many births, a ceaseless round,
I ran in vain, nor ever found
The Builder, though the house I saw, —
For death is born again, and hard the law.

O Builder, thou art seen! not so
Again thy building shall arise;
Broken are all its rafters, low
The turret of the mansion lies:
The mind in all-dissolving peace
Hath sunk, and out of craving found release.

C

O mother earth! O father air! O light,
My friend! O kindred water! and thou height
Of skies, my brother!— crying unto you,
    Crying, I plead adieu.

Well have I wrought among you, — now the day
Of Wisdom dawning strikes old Error's sway,
And the light breaks, and the long-waiting soul
    Greeteth her blissful goal.

www.ingramcontent.com/pod-product-compliance
Lightning Source LLC
Chambersburg PA
CBHW022137160426
43197CB00009B/1328